What Harvest

Also by Floyd Collins

Scarecrow

The Wedding Guest

Forecast

Seamus Heaney: The Crisis of Identity

Cover reproduction of José Arpa's *Funeral Pyre*
courtesy of the Alamo Museum.

What Harvest

Poems on the Siege & Battle of the Alamo

by
Floyd Collins

P.O. Box 3602 | Shepherdstown, West Virginia 25443

For information address Somondoco Press,
P.O. Box 3602, Shepherdstown, West Virginia 25443
www.somondocopress.com

First Edition

Printed in the United States of America.

ISBN 978-0-9789617-9-4

Book design by Brandon Cornwell, HBP Inc.

The poems in this collection, some in slightly different versions, first appeared or are forthcoming in the following publications:

Gettysburg Review: "James Bowie: Bexar, 1836"; "Travis"; "The Fruits of Victory"; "Alamo Pyre: March 6, 1836"; "San Antonio de Valero"; "Kentucky Long Rifles"; "Prelude to the Sandbar Duel: 1826"; "Bonham on the Night Prairie"; "Cannonade"; "Final Assault: Interlude"

Kenyon Review: "Kentucky Gunsmith: Long Rifle, 1833"; "Berserker"

Sewanee Review: "Degüello"; "Aftermath: Dawn at the Alamo"; "The Militia Shirt"; "Gregorio Esparza"; "Sighting the Vanguard"; "Santa Anna's Spurs"; "Aftermath: Dusk at the Alamo"; "The Natchez Sandbar Fight"; "Bonham *In Extremis*"

Shenandoah: "Crockett"; "Crockett By Firelight"

West Branch: "Eric Von Schmidt: Beyond Canvas"; "John McGregor (1808-1836)"; "Benjamin Rush Milam"

"James Bowie: Bexar, 1836" also appears in *Arkansas, Arkansas: Writers and Writings from the Delta to the Ozarks* (ed. John Caldwell Guilds, University of Arkansas Press, 1999).

"Bonham on the Night Prairie," "Crockett," "Prelude to the Sandbar Duel: 1826," and "Travis" also appear in *Lyric History: An Anthology of Poems about American History* (eds. Elizabeth Bradfield and Sean Hill, forthcoming).

"Santa Anna's Spurs" won the 2007 Allen Tate Poetry Prize from the *Sewanee Review.*

for Peter Stitt

Table of Contents

JAMES BOWIE: BEXAR, 1836

Into the chapel now withdrew the remnants of
the garrison. By most reports, Bowie himself was
sequestered in a side room, the baptistry.
Lon Tinkle, Thirteen Days to Glory

From the shoals of Bowie's blear-eyed fever
Wade the Aldama chasseurs, pompoms nodding
Above black leather shakos like cattails
Along the Louisiana bayou. Stretched a fort-
Night on his cot in the tiny baptistry
Of the mission church, San Antonio
De Valero, burned out by aguardiente
And a slow siege of tuberculosis,
For him this is *la hora de la verdad.*
Except to pry loose for melting and molding
Into bullets the little leaden filigree
Ornaments from the window casings
Of the limestone Alamo chapel,
The big knife shackled to his fist by turn
On turn of a black-beaded rosary
Has thus far played no part in the battle.

Bowie's chest labors like a ribbed bellows,
And again coals shift and glow white-hot
In the forge of James Black, Arkansas cutler
And smith who battered from a fantail of sparks
The huge blade now rinsed with a bluish luster.
A guttering tallow-dip in the dying man's cell,
Its walls stuccoed white and trimmed with azure,
Pinions the shadow of his propped shoulders
Like wings of a bat. Leather-stropped or

Sweetened on soapstone, his craving to cut
And slake with the cool Damascus was native
To the welter of youth. It gave him a handle,
The ivory-hafted steel, a slick purchase
On a rival's whole basket of guts.
Stacks of poker chips burst over the green
Felt gaming tables of Natchez-on-the-Hill

As he squandered a paper fortune hard-wrung
From bog-trotting, cypress, sugar cane, and rum.
Wed to Veramendi's daughter, a beauty
Intricate as the floral scroll carved above
The arched portal of this crumbling edifice,
Bowie yoked to his star the vice-governor's
Palace. But nothing stays in the province
Of Coahuila-Texas: land of scorpions,
Flint, and brick gouged out of yellow clay,
Each dwelling knows a subtle harmony
With earth, wind, and rain. Here *ancianos*
Weather the years like adobe, while cholera
Claims the young. Now Ursulita festers
In her shroud at Monclova, and the groom
Listens to the brass notes of the "Degüello"
Buckle in the predawn air. Pageantry

Attends death, as well as life, in Bexar.
Consider the chapel's sculpted façade,
How the passionate torque of each column
Squeezes out a Corinthian capital, a stone
Acanthus withered by frost and shellfire.
Enter the sanctuary, the inner walls
Spattered and pocked, thick plaster rippling
With shot from the massed *escopetas*:

Trace the rich stains at every station
Of the cross. What harvest is forthcoming
As he watches from the delirium,
Hoping to lure into his gleaming arc
An officer whose epaulettes and frogging
Drip silver? Sabbath sun streaks the bayonets,
And the brackish light begins to go.
Wind hushes in the cattails along the shore.

PRELUDE TO THE SANDBAR DUEL: 1826

When Jim Bowie confronted Norris Wright
In the taproom of Bailey's Inn for bruiting
His name about Rapides Parish in connection
With fraudulent land claims, the latter reached
Up his sleeve past an emerald cuff-button
For a small percussion-cap pistol and fired.
A low-grain charge with a heavy ball, the shot
Lodged in the dial plate of Bowie's watch.
Later, as he pried open the gold case,
The flywheel and tiny gears spilled out,
Minutely tooled trinkets, mere gimcrack
For the palm. A livid contusion and sore ribs
Were all the damage wrought. Henceforth,
Major Wright would live on borrowed time;
Not that Bowie begrudged him a ruptured
Timepiece. Nor was it the affront to honor,
The violation of the *code duello* in an age
When many a handsome young slab of a man
Cultivated his own scars, stark mementoes
Of the dueling grounds at Natchez and Chalmette,
Each imagining that deep-scored tissue
Lovingly traced by a lacquered nail
In a New Orleans boudoir. No, it was
The reckoning Bowie craved, the cruel
And irrevocable atonement face-to-face.
He could feel his hand fill with the haft
Of his lustrous blade, his heart quicken,
Gorging on enmity, the true life's blood.

THE NATCHEZ SANDBAR FIGHT

Though he cannot know it at such an hour,
This is Major Norris Wright's time to atone,
The final daybreak to take in certain ravishments
Of the eye and delectations of the ear: the music
Of a porcelain basin poured to the brim, a mauve-handled
Straight razor and frothing mug of mint-scented
Lather laid out for his morning's ritual laving
And whisking away of a night's crisp stubble.
He squires himself into silken white sleeves,
Securing each mother-of-pearl button
With the deftness of one who's master
Of the pasteboards, prestidigitator
Fanning a pat hand, spades and hearts,
A peacock beneath chandeliers spilling crystal
And nickel. Before quitting his chambers, he lifts
From a box two snub-nosed pistols slumbering in velvet,
Then reaches for his ivory-knobbed sword cane:
Jim Bowie would later gasp on the Natchez sandbar,
Sped through the lung with its slender yard
Of watery steel. But a terrible grip would close
On Wright's subtle wrist, his shoulder's bone-
Lappings keening as he strove to pull away. The
Interval was Bowie's. His whetted Damascus
Cut the major free of both liver and lights
There in the sun-stunned blaze of a delta noon,
The hour of no shadow when the wounded
And dead seem borne aloft on the gnat-swarming air,
And flocking sparrows grit up, filling their crops
With sweet sticky gobbets of warm sand.

TRAVIS

I. The Hewn Log House: Claiborne, Alabama

Hefting the steel-helved broadax for hours
Until a felled poplar was a beam hewn
Flush and smooth on four sides, a youth's
Torso slowly hardened into paneled oak.
The hollow gourd went to the barrel and back,
As Buck took his turn at a crosscut saw.
To avoid curling, cedar shakes were split
While the moon was on the wax, and peat moss
Culled for chinking drank many times
Its weight in moisture. Dovetail notches
Linked the logs at each corner. Creek stones
Bedded in lime mortar formed a chimney.
William Barret Travis lay by the fireplace,
Hearing salvos of bullfrogs and gators
Diminish along the starlit backwaters
Of Mobile. White-bellied mosquitos
Imbibed from his veins the sticky humors
As he dreamed a future written in blood.

II. Rough Justice

His clan traversed the wagon-rutted road
From Edgefield County, a South Carolina
Tract dubbed Pandaemonium or Abode
Of the Devils. By candlelight he got
A smattering of Latin and Greek,
Spilling more tallow in the loft by day
With Rosanna Cato. Married at nineteen,
Already he sat his black Spanish mare
Like a Cossack. Firing a sawed-off

Shotgun slung over his pommel kicked
The idle heart back to life: he loved the jolt
Of Anabaptist thunder, the sulfurous
Prickle that belled both nostrils. Spellbinder
And rhetorician, preferring the law
To the pulpit, one night he recast
Its letter in the shape of a spent ball.
He cited Rosanna's trifling, his skill
With a pistol, as reasons for a stranger's fall.

III. Command of the Alamo: February 24, 1836

His pen nib like a falcon's beak, horn-sheathed
And honed slick, seeking always to tap
The heart of the unborn republic, he scrawled
Bombast for an age of Byron and Scott
While the Mexican howitzers lobbed
Grenades into the compound: "To the People
Of Texas and all Americans in the World—."
So much for the quill-tip trimmed and slit,
The alchemy of words scripted in severe
Loops and swirls. He saw dragoons in brass
And steel glitter along the Alazan Heights,
Heard sappers' spades tongue gritty earth
As entrenchments nudged closer. A keepsake
For the dispossessed, his cat's-eye ring
Of beaten gold he threaded and dangled
About Angelina Dickinson's neck. Specters
Loomed in the tabernacle of his skull,
A votive nub winked in the chapel all night.

IV. The Final Assault: Five A.M., March 6, 1836

From the north battery, his cannon's spout
Spewed bits of chain and chopped horseshoes,
Wailing down rank on rank of the Toluca
Battalion. The cry of advancing columns
Shattered the empyrean, and he stood
Silhouetted one moment above the ramparts,
Hearing the syllables of his name leap
As he unsheathed the sabre at his side.
A blind volley broke the cluster of veins
At his temple, and he plummeted,
Brain-struck archangel, from the walls
Into grace: *"No rendirse, muchachos!"*
He called to men in Seguin's detachment
As the dull missile met his forehead,
Unsettling continents of bone. Where the hot
Lead cooled the blood congealed like wax.
His fate sealed, Travis saw the planet tilt,
Slow smoke unroll from the mission's rubble.

BONHAM ON THE NIGHT PRAIRIE

Deep gashes of vermilion and gold welter
Along the horizon; in the full onslaught
Of evening, James Butler Bonham
Drops a feral hog with one shoulder-shot
From his father's fifty-caliber Hawken—
Lacking time to unseam and field dress
The matted tusker, he carves out a haunch
With his Green River butcher knife,
And soon a cudgel of pork thigh
Crackles and spits as the fat runs
Over a fire of dry mesquite, bedded
Embers pulsing like stars in the night heavens.
What auspicious signs here converge,
As the weary Alamo courier stares
Into a veritable abyss of living coals,
Mindful of urgent missives that line
His deerskin saddlebags, appeals for aid
To Gonzales, Goliad, and San Felipe?
Thirty miles from San Antonio de Bexar,
He rode out when Mexican howitzers
Unlimbered and lobbed the first shells
Into the compound of sun-cured mud
And quarried limestone. Now utter silence
As lightning, viper tongued, licks around,
A storm or some other perilous
Circumstance amaking to the west,
Although the east is sprent with stars
And hope yet abides in its tiny settlements.
Bonham closes his eyes, once, twice—
Listens to his hobbled Appaloosa nicker

Only a few yards away, fang-bared wolves
Snarling in the distance over the boar's
Scattered entrails. Tomorrow he will clop
Into the dusty streets of Gonzales, but for now
He gazes deep within, seeking always
A portent, any nebulous glimmer
Still suspended in delicate equipoise
Amid the dark's listing firmament.
A meteor goes rifling down the void.

BONHAM *IN EXTREMIS*

Only in retrospect would the blood-dimmed
Outcome seem inevitable. And despite
The fact that the Mexican generalissimo
Set snapping on the afternoon breeze,
From a makeshift staff atop the belfry
Of bronze-domed San Fernando, a red
Skull and crossbone-blazoned banner
Of no quarter, we were never men bent
On the main chance, and took all such
Blackguards for callow, comic-opera
Buffoons who loved a jest. Yet the boldest
Among us stared a spell at the line Travis
Traced deep in the caliche soil at our feet
Before seized by any impulse to step
Out of the quotidian flesh and into history,
Where the courtyard gathered us close,
Knitting us ghost and sinew in one resolve.
And, indeed, among us one Louis Rose
Chose to slip over the west wall, nettles
From a field of nopal that he blundered
Into somewhere out there near sundown
Pricking more deeply than conscience.
Buck kept in the pocket over his heart
A letter from "Three-Legged" Willie
Saying filibusters rallied at San Felipe,
Dismissing Fannin and the truculence
That refused to let him budge a half-
Mile beyond La Bahía's stronghold.
I myself carried the fateful dispatch, riding
From settlement to presidio in weather

Both parched and torrential, the hoofprints
Of my Appaloosa oozing shut behind me.
We woke before daylight next morning
To the sound of one bugle taken up
And swelled to the swart Moorish tones
Of the "Degüello," the regimental bands
Urging the Centralist battalions forward.
Soon but a few gunners held the platform
High in the apse of the Alamo church.
We swung about a brass six-pounder,
Plugging the bore with langrage, chopped
Horseshoes and nails; Esparza set linstock
To priming tube, the hoarse report
And rising gust of incandescent metal
Ripping an even dozen Matamoros
Grenadiers to tatters. Thronging *soldados*
Regrouped inside the chapel's archway,
And muskets banked like galley oars,
Each rank fired volley after volley, bayonets
Gleaming phosphor. Smoothbore shot
Plinked off the mortared limestone interior,
Leaden spheroids spent beyond flesh and bone.
I lay riddled and blood-boltered on the scaffold,
My last breath a wisp unfurling the dawn air.

ALAMO PYRE: MARCH 6, 1836

Soldiers layered the pyres with wood and kindling,
then bodies, then more wood, kindling, and bodies.
Jeffery Long, *Duel of Eagles*

Like brightly plumed fighting cocks in a pit,
The first flames to crest the pyre buffet and flap,
Fall back. Stacked northeast of La Villita,
Scrub oak and mesquite in layers, then
A row of corpses, a few bled so white
Their bones shine like ivory tapers lit
Beneath the vaulted dome of San Fernando.
No incantation here, not even the *rogus* of pagan Rome:
This is the heretic's fire steepled, forking
Here and there among the branches
Of hacked and splintered chaparral. Crockett's
Buckskin fringe sizzles, then twines blue smoke
Like a cache of duds. Heat begins to raze
The lightly downed cheek of Carlos Espalier:
Protégé to Bowie, on feast days he rode
Down Calle Durango like an emperor
Bestowing on all the imperial nod.
After the battle, the Vera Cruz fusiliers
Sheared from his leggings the silver buttons,
Stripped his leather boots of the gringo spurs.
Before daybreak they had riddled out
His life's mystery at bayonet point;
Now the fire sputters and pops, feeding
His resinous heart. The sticky sap
Seethes in his loins; tendons and cartilage

Whine as the bones pull apart. Santa Anna
Paces in a striped marquee, waiting to crush
Beneath his heel the last filibuster spark.

CROCKETT

The Colonel had found an old fiddle somewhere, and he
would challenge McGregor to get out his bagpipes to see
who could make the most noise.
Walter Lord, *A Time to Stand*

The coonskin cap some purists vow he never wore
Bristles in firelight as he carves out
On his fiddle a Celtic air, and the little
Ring-tailed scrapper gone blind with the rage
Of gazing inward emblazons the span
Above his brow. In the shadow of the slab-
Sided chapel, a spitted ox bastes and seethes,
Cornbread crackles in an iron skillet. Crockett
Surrendered, they now say, and Santa Anna's
Gleaming entourage cut him down as tailors
Would a legend grown too large. The steel
Was still smoking when they resheathed
The swords with basket-hilts of inlaid silver.
Mrs. Dickinson would later remember
His corpse amid the other carnage
In the courtyard, how the "peculiar cap"
Lay by Crockett's side. Whether or not
Its glossy nap yet stirred with the deathless
Saga of the Canebrake Congressman is unknown—
But conjure him once, his face stained
With the low-banked fires of the Alamo plaza,
The fiddle braced under his chin, the slender
Arm dancing out and in, while McGregor's pipes
Bleat like newborn kids on a swollen udder.

CROCKETT BY FIRELIGHT

To thwart the evening chill, John Crockett
Would draw a deep tankard of his own stock
From an oak-staved cask. A leather-aproned
Tavern host grown stout with the memory
Of wielding the flintlock pegged above the bar
At the battle of King's Mountain, he often
Took the measure of his stripling son
With a birch rod. Young David never chafed

At splitting fence rails with maul and wedge,
But when his father sent him to scratch
A slate at the age of twelve, he bolted.
Now he hunkers by firelight in the chalk-white
Glow of the limestone chapel, his name
A legend in columns back East. An iron horse
Hitched to a congregation of vapors,
The *Davy Crockett* beats its way

From Saratoga to Schenectady
Belching a cloud of sparks. Crockett closes
His eyes a moment, rides the cool
Slipstream of twenty-five miles an hour
Beneath the stars of the old republic.
Yet he prefers the tall chestnut mare
With the blaze on her forehead. She bore
His raw-boned bulk from Gibson County

To San Antonio, helped him escape
The industrial reek of the seaboard states,
Whig intrigue, the glib political
Machine of Jackson's Kitchen Cabinet,

Inexorable gears that notch and wheel,
Grinding the common man to bonemeal.
Stump oratory came easy at first,
Each ballot like a glimmering perch

Snatched from a millrace with the hook
Of native wit. But Crockett's constituency
Went straight to hell at the August polls.
Before the ripe persimmons fumed
In a killing frost and the black bear gorged,
He struck out for Texas, the bluestem prairies
Rolling away under the hooves of buffalo.
He forsook "Pretty Betsey," the engraved

Pennsylvania rifle inlaid with gold
And German silver, a weapon shaped
By the gods of covetousness. He chose
Instead his percussion muzzle-loader,
Its copper nipple, and the smoke-smudged
Sights that gleam no warning. Tonight
He fed his fire in the Alamo courtyard
A shoot of resinous cedar; an ember popped,

Leapt the flames, and lit like a flea on the toe
Of his boot: "Lice and such varmints as these
Always quit a dying man," he observed,
"I'm good for a few years yet." Others roared,
But he swallowed like it was hard medicine.
A seraphic ghoul resplendent in frock coat
And bullion tassels, Santa Anna offered
A battalion of *fusileros* for slaughter

Nine days ago. How many yeoman-crowned
Bullhide shakos did Crockett topple
Between the mud-chinked *jacales* south
Of the mission outworks? Before the sun
Turns the evening mist to blood-red dawn,
He foresees a full-scale assault. A torch
Spindles and wisps near the low barracks wall.
Women and children dream on burnished straw.

GREGORIO ESPARZA

Although a member of Seguin's company, Esparza helped
man a cannon in the Alamo chapel where his wife and
children were sheltered.
William Groneman, *Alamo Defenders*

At the cusp of summer, amid mayflies,
Herons patrol the reedy, milk-jade shallows
Of the San Antonio, their necks recurved
Bows darting at minnows. Tomatoes,
Squash, onions, figs, wild mustang grapevines
Thrive in Gregorio Esparza's garden.
On the acequia's east bank, his two-room
Adobe breathes with the earth, its cool,
Dry interior hung with strings of red
And yellow peppers: "Of food, we had
Not overmuch—beans and chile, chile
And beans...but there was time to work and rest
And look at growing plants." Winter grips
Bexar, effacing the arid landscape,
And the hairy hand of a tarantula
Fiddles at the latch. Dolorous hooves
Toll along the stony Camino Real,
As Santa Anna's mounted vanguard
Enters the barren Northern provinces
Like a cold wind from Ecclesiastes.

In February, the Centralist eagles
Cross the Medina: Esparza casts his lot
With the insurgents in the old mission,
Hoisting by rope and pulley onto a scaffold

In the apse of the church a terrible
Deus ex machina, the iron tube
Of a Spanish twelve-pounder adorned
With twin dolphins. Thirteen days he abides
Aloft this makeshift ramp. His *niño* Enrique
Shrinks from flames, the crumping roar
Of the three-piece battery. Like Dickinson,
He keeps wife and children close,
Fingering his beads on the rainy evening
When Juan Seguin lays his scourge
Against the racing flanks of Bowie's sorrel,
And vanishes down the Gonzales road.
The big knife-fighter, Don Santiago,
Tosses on a cot in the low barracks:
Leeches batten on the fever in his blood.
Doc Pollard drags hard, sears them off

With the smoldering ash of a cigar.
Esparza's cannon broaches the night air,
And as sparks shower the platform,
He knows how futile his attempt
To break the generalissimo's hold.
The siege tightens; a mineral sweat
Lurks in the limestone walls by day,
Making the chapel dank as a sepulchre.
Catcalls drift across the river each twilight,
Words so serenely murderous they
Raise the hackles at Gregorio's nape.
He sees men crouch around watchfires
In the Alamo compound, silence
And shadow the only realities

During a lull. One Anglo knocks lead
From a pincer mold, another whets
An Arkansas toothpick on the sole
Of his boot. Like a peasant girl
From her rebozo, the moon peers down.
The assault columns edge into place.

SOLILOQUY OF JOHN M. HAYS

It's a fitful sleep we sleep this March five
Evening in the eighteen-hundred and thirty-sixth
Year of Grace, the Mexican cordon silent,
A constricting serpent poised in its glittering
Toils about the Alamo's mudbrick redoubts—
A gust whistles up our dying watchfire,
Blue embers shed flakes of flame downwind...
A later age will claim that I and others
Of Bowie's company lay so this chill night
Because the San Saba silver lurked deep
In the shaft of the old mission's dry well,
That no high-souled courage born of despair
Kept us here at our appointed stations.
Not so, but I've a stranger tale to tell.
Back home in the Tennessee woodland
My young cousin owned a brooch richer
Than the King Alfred jewel, and she asked
As consumption sunk her day by day
Into the semblance of bone and socket,
That the ornament be clasped at her throat
When we laid her to rest. We knocked
Together a coffin with fitted dowel pins,
Caulked like any skiff and still sweating
Resin, before turning aside a creek
With field stones, mud, and the detritus
Of last autumn's leaves. We delved it seems
Twelve feet down in the clay bed, lowered
Her pine box, refilled the grave, and turned
The waters back into their wonted course.

Is it light on that moon-dazed current
Or my own fretful muttering keeps me
On the verge of waking as an elf owl yelps,
Mounting high above the ruined walls
And bosky arroyos of our final reckoning?

KENTUCKY LONG RIFLES

In the buttstock of polished maple,
A hinged cavity hid the greasy, square-cut
Linen patches that wrapped each leaden ball,
Easing it along spiral grooves engraved
The barrel's length. Tamped home against
A sixty grain charge, the snug fit between slug
And rifling formed a gas seal, boosting
Pressure and velocity. From dun walls
On the sunrise side of the river, a poised
Sniper could spill the eye of a gold-braided
Zapadore at two hundred paces. Saxon
Gutturals lit the powder train when flint
Kissed steel, and many a rebel lived
An eternity in the abrupt snarl
And flare of the hangfire. His jaw
Swollen with a quid of tobacco,
Admiring the clean-run, equestrian
Grace of Sesma's dragoons, Crockett
Sighted along the earth-rammed palisade
Between the chapel and low barracks,
Squeezing off round after round. Twelve days
The Army of Operations kept a distance
From the Alamo's crumbling redoubts.
Silver cartwheels rang every night
In the *pulquerías* and brothels,
Candles spent like profligates in reed-
Thatched *jacales* east of town. Violin,
Guitar, and cornet: eleven evenings
Of revelry, though Kentucky long rifles
Showed His Excellency each morning
How Texas cut the pigeon's wing.

KENTUCKY GUNSMITH: LONG RIFLE, 1833

Blacksmith, mechanic, wood-sculptor, jeweler:
He begins in the forge, wrapping a pressed bar
Of wrought iron braced on a swage block
With ringing triple skelps of his hammer
Around a mandril rod. He sinks the lap-welded
Barrel in a ticking bed of gold and blue
Bituminous embers, letting it cool
And set before he wrests the metal free
With tongs and bears it smoking like hoarfrost
To the anvil, where he batters out the flats,
Eight sides, up and down its length.
He bores smooth the octagonal tube, then rifles it—
Hickory shims set behind steel cutting teeth
Deepen the grooves with each successive pass.

He fashions lock and plate piece by piece.
Consigning frizzen, fly, tumbler, and springs
To the crucible, he threads the breechplug
And draws the glowing tang sharp as a prong:
A forked vein pulses in his temple,
His eyes glaze and crack with blood.
Before sand-casting both muzzle-cap
And buttplate in brass, he retrieves
And quenches the parts of tempered steel.
The heat-refracted shed recedes
Like a mirage, as he walks sixteen furlongs
To the Morgan Whitehackle Inn.
The tavern host slides a tall schooner
Of amber-lit ale across the polished board.

Thoughts steeped in seasoned grains, he savors
The barley-bree, mulling texture and hue,
Chopped heartwood of curly maple
Planed smooth with a drawknife. He returns
To the shop, traces on a cured slab the rude
Template of his stock. His gouge and drill-bit
Drop ringlets and curls. He cuts the lugs,
Seats the barrel, tests the ramrod groove.
Rasp and file embalm the air, as he raises
Cheekpiece and comb on the buttstock.
He endows the wrist with a slender turn,
Chisels a rib to secure lock, cock, frizzen,
And ignition pan. He blocks out a cavity
For the springworks, assembles the hardware,

And next a pillar of blazing sawdust motes
He starts to carve in earnest. Virtuosity
In the pursuit of form lies in slickest
Evasion. Everything flows, sinuous
Lines holding plane and mass forever
In the present tense. The stock tapers
And flares all the barrel's length. He raises
In low relief a baroque C-scroll behind
The cheekpiece. Above the vent-pick eyelets,
He incises a garfish and taps the glyph
Full of relic silver. He chases
Rime-encrusted florals, stars, and sickle moons
Along the tang and breech. He files
Diamond facets into the ramrod thimbles

And redeems in linseed oil the sculpture's
Tiger-striped grain. Spurning always
The nacreous tints of fresh-water pearl,

For inlay he chooses ivory worried
From the jawbone of Pleistocene cave bear,
Ferocious canines arcing slow meteors
Either side of the forestock. Thirty months
The sun fails beautifully on beaten sheet brass,
The hinged patch box cunningly embellished
As a gilt frame in a New Orleans parlor—
Until Daniel William Cloud, 24 years old,
Bound for rebellion in the Texas province,
Puts down ten Coronet gold eagles, swings up
By the left stirrup, and boots his horse toward Bexar.

·

SIGHTING THE VANGUARD

Red-jacketed and brass-gleaming, astraddle
Nickering mustangs, Sesma's dragoons crest
The Alazan hills. The horsemen advance
Their guidons, tack and bit-chains rattling, lance tips
Contending with light. A tatterdemalion
Sentry squints back from his post aloft
The San Fernando belfry. Oleander
Spices the frosty forenoon air of Bexar,
Where the motley garrison lies snoring
After last night's fandango, a flurry
Of peaked tortoise-shell combs
And sequined fans, Crockett grinning
Like Old Scratch over his canted fiddle.
Unshaven, haggard from lack of sleep,
The lookout recoils and glances due east
Across the Main Plaza at the meandering
San Antonio, then toward the mission-fortress
Beyond. The limestone Alamo chapel
Seems to dazzle with a desolate beauty
There in the ashen glare of February sun.
How hard the light breaks in a time
When all firearms, even fowling-pieces,
Are charged by muzzle, ignited by flint
Gleaned from the mineral soil, refuge
Of the golden skink and horned toad.
Temples pounding with his first hangover,
Robert Brown seizes the bell rope
And pulls to rouse the slumbering men.

CANNONADE

The sun's warm benefice thaws brittle frost,
A glaze of lacy ferns and white flowers
Melting in a slather down cottage panes.
Such memories of autumn in the Ozarks—
Trees ablaze with color, the townships
Borne along by the masque and pageant
Of the turning season. Now it is winter
In Bexar, and Henry Warnell leaves off
The felicitous dolor of his musings,
Watches the mud dauber building
Its organ stacks high in the roofless ruin
Of the mission church Valero. Soon
Mexican howitzers dug in across the river
Lob hissing grenades bursting orange
Against the west-wall footings; cannon
Hurling solid shot threaten to pulverize
A timber-shored section of the Alamo's
North bastion. Blue haze and the stink
Of sulfur hover over the plaza, recalling
To Warnell the spider that lit in his skillet
At breakfast, how the little spinner
Scrambled up a strand of smoke
And disappeared. Jockey and horse thief,
An honest man when he feels like it,
He swears by ill omens: hammered
Into his left boot heel a cross of nails
Wards off the devil and all trumpery imps.
The Centralist cannoneers retire at dusk,
Wash faces creased black with their trade
In the blessed plenitude of the San Antonio.

SANTA ANNA'S SPURS

for George Core

I. Mexico City: the Street of the Artisans, 1834

Not the hammer with its deft sure stroke,
But the anvil, blue-black as a meteorite,
Rings home the shaping of steel. The smith, by dint
Of sheer will, forges from hoar-white metal
Heel, shank, and rowel, the spur perfect
For quickening the glossy flanks of any stallion,
Putting the proudest horseflesh on its mettle.
This is the Calle Plateros, Mexico City,
Circa 1834. *El Presidente* seeks out
An artisan of yet finer touch, desiring
For the heel a gold-inlaid band exquisitely
Engraved with trailing vines. Next he locates
A man that knows the raw whiff and burn
Of everyday toil, a craftsman who works
In hand-tooled leather; Santa Anna wants
Straps he can wear buckled on the inside
To show off conchos of purest silver.

*   *

II. San Antonio de Bexar: March 5–6, 1836

Against the backdrop of a westering sun
Almost lost behind the Alazan Heights,
Each radiant of the generalissimo's rowel
Suddenly flares as the man himself is cast
Into silhouette; the drawn moderation
Of his lean profile belies the caprice

That will crush beneath his boot heel,
Like a dirt clod, the adobe battlements
Of the Alamo before dawn.
                              In darkness,
Around watchfires, rebels of determined mien
Run balls and cut patches for long rifles—
They grease little swatches of cloth
In fat fleeced from slaughtered steers,
Cross-notch each leaden orb so it shatters
Human bone on impact. Soon come
The fiery strains of the "Degüello,"
The flames' liquefaction and crackling
Among thatched hovels along the west wall.
Rank on rank, fusils level and ignite,
Spouting sulfurous jets, as Mexican battalions
Carry the compound with shot and bayonet.

First light hardens to translucent horn
In the silent chancel of the roofless church.
Maimed *soldados* lie in field hospitals
Calling out for *Maria, Madre de Dios*;
Captain Juan Sanchez-Navarro avers,
"Another such victory will ruin us."

                    *   *

III. Mexico City: September, 1847

Big-rowelled spurs: the mark of the *caballero*.
Santa Anna cannot do other than hearken
To the tingle and whir of his booted striding
Down corridors of state. This morning,
He must surrender to General Winfield Scott,
Who returns his sword worth seven thousand pesos.

Not to be outdone, gesture for gesture,
The *caudillo* unbuckles and bestows
His gold-mounted spurs on the grizzled *norte*.
Pride in his estate called Manga de Clavo—
Spike of the Clove at red-tiled Jalapa—
And his fighting cocks of burnished feather,
Clings like a burr for years to come.

        *   *

IV. Mexico City, 1847 - Appomattox, 1865

Scott broods on the spurs' gilt pattern,
Imagining a dew-soaked vineyard fanning out
Like the first rays of sun. He remembers
Mexico City's great cathedral, its
Soaring vaults and silver altar rails,
The carved *santos*, their painted robes
Set with rubies, sapphires, and topaz—
Beneath loose wooden floorboards lay
Old corruption and dead men's bones,
The mingling of magnificence and squalor
To Scott's Protestant reckoning a legacy
Of priest-vested despots down the ages.

The general sits at his portable escritoire,
An alabaster lamp laps oil. Caring little
For the spoils of war, he will award the spurs
To Benjamin Huger, his youthful captain
Of ordnance and artillery, citing valor
At Vera Cruz, Chapultepec, Molino del Rey.

The spurs become heirlooms when Huger
Presents them to his son on graduation
From West Point. Officer in the Norfolk
Light Artillery, Frank Huger stands by his brass
Smoothbore Napoleons at Fredericksburg,
Reaping the advancing Federal lines
With grapeshot and canister. Captured
Near Appomattox, he lends the spurs
To his old classmate, George Armstrong Custer—
Thus they fall into the hands of another cavalier.

      *   *

V. The Little Big Horn: June 25, 1876

Custer delights in each chinking heel-strike,
Deems the spurs fit plunder for a brigadier,
And forgets the staid gunner with whom
He shared a sterling hip flask at the Point.

Like Santa Anna, he owns the habit
Of contempt, mistaken for flamboyance
By those who admire his navy blue tunic
And flowing red cravat, the buckskin jacket

Worn despite the swelter and haze, his brow
Popped with sweat beneath a Montana sun.
Rolling drums and skirling fifes brazen out
"Garry Owen," making his scalp go taut

And prickle as he goads his sorrel forward—
The swallow-tailed guidons of the Seventh
Flutter and snap. The regimental band stays
At Powder River Depot; all sabres have been

Crated up and the pine lids nailed shut.
No martial airs or clanking steel must alert
The Sioux and Northern Cheyennes. Crow scouts
Spy a vast herd of grazing ponies and warn

The Son of the Morning Star—how he relishes
The epithet—to look for "worms in the grass."
He plunges down Medicine Tail Coulee,
And strikes the middle of a sprawling camp

Two miles long, his last message a scrawl:
"Benteen. Big village. Be quick. Bring packs."
Five companies perish among the hills
And gullies, Custer's ivory-handled

English Webley bulldogs banging off
Cylinder after cylinder before he falls,
A rifle ball lodged under his ribcage.
He lies back, amazed by a painted arrow's

Slow arc, the ecstatic hover and plummet
To earth, like a hawk stooping on its prey.
As his grey eyes film and his gaze dries,
He has no thought for the Alamo garrison

Burned to glory on mass pyres forty years ago,
Or the *caudillo*, dead just three weeks past,
Returned from exile to Mexico, his last days
Lived out, serene, in solitude and poverty.

THE FRUITS OF VICTORY

Halley's comet: the year of the broom-star.
Santa Anna swept the northern provinces
Clear of homesteaders within twelve months.
Saddle-notched dogtrot cabins, hewn heartwood
Blazed in Gonzales till the least ember
Hissed to a standstill amid charred wreckage.

Nearer the Sabine, barns burst with cotton
Ginned and carded; bludgeons of pork thigh
Swung from smokehouse rafters, bacon slabs
Carved thick as psalters cured in a cryptic blue.
Plunder was abundant: beeswax, white sugar,
Bitter chocolate, mirrors, clocks, whiskey.

One-fourth of the Toluca Battalion
Leavened the sunbaked graves at Bexar.
That frozen, cirrus-misted night in March
They had perished by the squad as Travis's
Cannon bucked, hurling shrapnel from the north-
West wall. The Campo Santo could not hold

Their sum. Corpses drifted in the suck
And sway as the purling San Antonio made
Crisp gashes breathe like gills. Santa Anna
Pondered stippled trout, the hummingbirds
Of the South. From the lava-rich tropics
To the high chaparral, he embodied it all.

Green rind, white quick, red core—like a silken
Tricolor—watermelon would split open
At one swift stroke of the *caudillo*'s sword.
He dreamed of his estates at Jalapa,
El Presidente, dozing in his pavilion
While the columns groped toward San Jacinto.

DEGÜELLO

Islamic Moors first sounded the "cut-throat" song
In Spain, its fiery strains recasting each bugle
In tones of molten brass. It summoned death
And decay, the mephitic vapors of a wound
Left untended for days. When Santa Anna's
Regimental bands swelled the Mexican advance,
The Texas hardpan quaked like an Arab drum,
The Alamo fell to the glint of fixed bayonets.
Scored notes: grenadiers marching *en punto*.
Dawn trumpet bleeding down the gauze-streaked sky.

FINAL ASSAULT: INTERLUDE

His ruby-meated heart like a fist kneads
The rich arterial blood into every sinew,
And for the moment Daniel Bourne is more
Than antic clay doomed to fall clod cold

On the gun ramp mounting the south-
West corner of the Alamo's dun walls.
From Mexican batteries to the north,
Congreve rockets hiss and explode

In the predawn haze; the regimental bands
Massed beyond air the Moorish "Degüello"
With the fierce somnolence of flies brassily
Swarming ripe viscera in a slaughter pen.

Firing on the precipice of each plumed breath,
Bourne feels his rifle barrel heat up
Like an ax bit, and when a tallow-
Greased patch wrapping a lead ball sizzles

As he tamps it home with his ramrod,
He knows measuring another fifty-grain charge
Of black powder would be folly. Abruptly,
He quits his post on the outer perimeter

And crosses the compound to the barracks
Of plaster-flaked limestone, searching
His saddlebags for a cheroot that he lights
Off a pistol flint, nurturing the brief spark to life.

For a long minute he savors the smooth
Virginia tobacco, before he takes up
A short-fused grenade in either hand,
Recrosses the plaza, and climbs the berm.

The smoldering cigar proves the ideal punk
For the lethal pomegranates Bourne drops
Among the Aldama *cazadores*, who even
Now place their scaling ladders and ascend

To take soundings in his chest with bared steel,
The rebel's aorta pelting the muddy slope—
Gouts that cool and set like obsidian
Gleaming icily in the frost fires of morning.

ERIC VON SCHMIDT: BEYOND CANVAS

In Von Schmidt's *The Storming of the Alamo*,
It's a half-hour since the trumpets brayed
Columns of *soldados*, crouched in a dark field
Of trampled maize, to their feet and forward
To the north wall of glazed, shell-pocked adobe
Braced by packed earth and rough-shorn timbers.
Pumped into a sky still popped with stars,
Flares illuminate the plaza as William Carey
Gouges with the vent-pick on his thumb
The powder bag rammed fast to the breech
Of his cannon, and drives a priming tube
Into the charge. Coiled with a slow fuse,
No doubt his twinkling linstock trembles
Grafting fire to black grain. The big gun rolls,
Disgorging into the Aldama Battalion twelve pounds
Of searing iron links. Caught in a flank maneuver,
The field manual's smart right oblique,
Did *los jovenes* remember the camp gypsy,
The gut-thumping membrane, the quick sizzle
Of her tambourine, as the shrapnel
Cut a swath through their serried ranks?
But the elite *Zapadores* climb up
The patched redoubt, its chinks and uneven
Beam ends, spilling over onto the parapet.
Carey pauses to crush with a handspike
The temporal bone beneath a dragoon's
Helmeted brow. The acrid snap and tongued flame
Of a smoothbore ignite his woolen jacket—
Like knives at a spit, the bayonets probe.

JOHN MCGREGOR (1808–1836)

I

Lightning puts a seam in a dark cloud mass
On the horizon beyond La Villita
Where company officers fire *Arribas!*
At the line troops of Battalion Matamoros,
Staccato accents opposing teeth and tongue
Like flint and steel. McGregor bites off
A twist of tobacco, and muttering
His "God damn ye" through the cured leaf,
Frames a shot with his Spanish *tercerola.*
Several volleys from the lunette battery
Fronting the Alamo's main gate
Mingle with stipplings of cold rain,
And the Mexicans retire in disarray.
It's 11:00 a.m., February twenty-five,
Ten days before the final assault.

II

If the Scotsman's earthwork station
Lacks the reliquary grace of the chapel's
Hand-hewn limestone, its moat and palisade
Hold fast in the predawn gloom of March sixth,
When he touches a sputtering linstock
To the powder vent of a bronze eight-pounder—
Out in the darkness beyond the ditch,
Hail shot rings on polished metal plate,
Rips clean through the black leather shell
Of a dragoon's helmet; the encased skull,
Bursting like a ripe pomegranate, fouls

The peaked horsehair comb with spattered gore.
Grenadiers swarm the southwest barbette,
Forcing McGregor to break for the chaparral,
Where lances inflict deckle-edged wounds.

III

Carrion hawks and snot-knobbed vultures
Circle the carefully tiered funeral pyres
That smolder on the Alameda, north and south,
For two days. Suppose nothing now remains
Of McGregor save charred bones, human suet,
And a few buttons stamped in brass? Among
Thickets of mesquite thorn below the old mission

A diamondback sloughs its skin like an argyle sock.

BERSERKER

Acrid fumes of charred brimstone
Assail the thronging San Luis *cazadores*
As they clamber up timbers bracing
The Alamo's shell-eroded north wall.

Colonel Amat's sappers attack with pick
And crowbar the lime-washed adobe bricks
That now seal the west-facing window
Of the Trevino house. Exhorting others

To follow, a young officer, his tunic front
Scintillant as a glockenspiel, vaults
The sepia-toned rubble. It proves
Daunting to fall back, to seat with sweat-

Crawling palms a lead ball in a muzzle-loader.
Northcross unbuckles his shotgun belt,
Strips the packed leather tube from his back—
Plugging in turn each barrel with a brass spout

He wrings the pellets home like a butcher
Pouring gravel from a goose's crop.
Cocking and leveling, he blasts a fusilier
Heaving a gleaming short sword

From under his shako's yellow raquettes
And cording. Sternum shattered and ribcage
Sprung, the luckless *soldado* never hears
The sleeting double thump. He closes his eyes

On candescent barrels roiling like blowflies.
Someone bellows in a dark corner
Of the mission's long barracks, a man
Who has earned the bear-shirt, the berserker's

Keening blood-wail; he flails enrapt
The burst crown of his empty powder horn,
Smashing jaws hard-set and crammed with molars,
Rupturing the frail sutures of every skull.

THE MILITIA SHIRT

Even as the Gonzales Ranging Company
Set out for the Alamo on the afternoon
Of February 27, 1836, fifteen-year-old
William Phillip King caught the reins
Of Captain Kimball's nutmeg roan
And begged leave to go in his father's stead.
He had nine younger siblings. Let someone
Sturdier follow the double yoke of oxen
Pulling the long furrow toward sundown.
Kimball shrugged; his rump firmly settled
In the hull of a new Ringgold saddle,
He nodded reluctant assent, his long rifle's
Feather-grained cherrywood riding
Easy in the crook of his arm. King's mother
Had nightmares all the coming week:
The old mission chapel's ornate façade
Obscured in the particle haze and sulfurous
Reek of powdersmoke, her firstborn
Fighting for his life with a Green River
Butcher knife rehafted in elkhorn. Every day
Her spinning wheel ran with the sun,
And each night she sat at her loom
Weaving threads into whole fabric.
She had cut and sewn the chamber-dyed
Militia shirt, biting back loose strands
Like cries of grief. Now she saw a *cazadore*'s
Double-edged sword bayonet burst
The fascia of William's abdomen,
Glutinous red drink the rough butternut
Cloth of linen warp and woolen weft.

AFTERMATH: DAWN AT THE ALAMO

Some still stabbed at the corpses with their bayonets
and here and there fired a shot, so overwrought by
the fight or the loss of comrades that even vengeance
against a dead foe seemed to help.

William C. Davis, *Three Roads to the Alamo*

In the breast pocket of a slain defender
Impaled against the wall by a bayonet thrust,
A slim gold watch chimes the hour:
Blood percolating through chill limestone.
A young sapper's hand, brown and hardened
By the toil of hefting retrenchment tools,
Seizes the precious heirloom. Who
Could have divined that the slumped figure,
Face hidden by a broad-leafed Spanish
Hat of svelte beaver, the ribbed vault of his torso
Wrapped in a blanket coat with dark blue
Selvage binding, would yield such a trove?
The Texian never unsheathed his massive
Sheffield bowie, but the left hand still
White-knuckles a pistol's cross-hatched grip,
Coveting the flintlock's silver butt-cap,
The barrel chased with scroll and floral motifs.
The *soldado* resists the impulse to remove
The broad brimmed hat, level his *escopeta*
At the blond head, and replaster with brains
The barrack wall. Already dawn colors
The horizon east of the smoldering Alamo.
Such stains, indelible, run deep enough.

AFTERMATH: DUSK AT THE ALAMO

John Purdy Reynolds sprawls before the chapel's
Blood-spattered façade, its earth tones
Of burnt umber and raw sienna no longer
Beguiling his every glance. Indeed the town
Of San Antonio, the white-washed adobes
And dwellings of hewn limestone, conjured
For many a footloose garrison bravo
A New World Judea. A little beyond the river,
Sun-spangled at the gravel-barred ford,
Stood the shantytown of La Villita with its onyx-
Eyed *señoritas*; here the fare was often plain—
Tamales wrapped in cornshucks, pulque
Sipped from jars of unfired clay—but each night
Reynolds lay in one girl's casual embrace,
Moonlight seeping through the chinked *jacale*,
A cricket in the thatch like a bell of black tin.
Now an ashen haze has settled over the mission
This chill sabbath, and his Kentucky-wrought
Smokepole no longer shoots for gold braid.
In the lapel of his blue swallow-tailed coat
Hot lead spun off the lands and grooves
Of a Baker rifle fired from the west wall
Left a boutonnière of caked blood
Where the fatal round plunked home.
Straight as a bride, a solitary figure moves
Among the rebels in the hour before twilight,
Seeking out one soul of all the dead:
From a countenance curiously serene
She wipes thick battle-grime and flecked gore,
Placing the soaked kerchief between her breasts.
Tumbrils groan, rolling corpses to bonfires.

BENJAMIN RUSH MILAM

He cast a numinous eye along creekbeds,
Sand and gravel bars for the least glimmer
Of flint, chert, agate or hard jasper,
Any stone that would strike a spark
From the steel frizzen of his long rifle.
He stalked deer in all seasons, fringed
Buckskins breaking up his silhouette
As he stole through the cane. He loved the double-
Jointed click of a hammer thumbed back
To full lock. Flash-point of the assault
That seized Bexar in December, 1835,
On the third day he fell brainshot,
Limbs wracked and battered by spasms,
In the yard of the Veramendi house. Buried
On the spot in a hexagonal "toe-pincher,"
His Masonic ring pocketed by a thief
When officials exhume the coffin years later,
Milam is reinterred in a Protestant
Sector across from the Campo Santo.
His chiseled sepulchre tablet, furred
With moss, crumbles like blue cheese
As the decades pass, his remains lost,
Until a Bobcat backhoe turns up
Rotting boards and several vertebrae
Leached frail as pumice by groundwater.
Forensic evidence shows he was somewhat
Shorter than the bronze six-footer
That brandishes a rifle in the park named
For the grizzled veteran, the plaque's
Legend immutable: "Who'll go
Into San Antonio with old Ben Milam?"

SAN ANTONIO DE VALERO

I. The Mission Period: Antonio de Tello

In the Year of Our Lord, seventeen hundred
And fifty-six, master artisan
Antonio de Tello, having served
A full apprenticeship peeling limestone
With mallet and chisel, carving rosettes,
Grape clusters, acres of gothic fretwork,
Having observed the heresies of the Moorish
Influence right down to a snail's tiny mosque,
Gathers his well-honed tools and sets off
For the province of *Tejas*, there to transpose
The façade of the mission chapel
Near the reed-choked banks of the San Antonio
From a frowning mass to a marvel
Of Tuscan form. Yet the good friars

Care less for high artifice than the souls
Of *los Yndios Reducidos*. The curate
Locks pubescent converts, male and female,
Into separate cells every night
With eagle-headed keys of cold iron.
Several millennia before, sparks leapt
As rapacious Apaches chipped free
A new ballistics slumbering in the core
Of igneous rock; now the adobe walls
And rough-hewn pueblos of the compound
Thwart the heathen's obsidian-tipped arrows.
Antonio waits two years for the ornate
Keystone to be set and blessed. After all,
Sculpture is an art of subtraction: better add

Stripe upon stripe to the backs of neophytes
Than cut twisted columns from the west
Face of the brooding Alamo. His St. Clare
Betrays in each contour the nubile grace
Of an onyx-eyed girl who grinds maize
In the kitchens. The scallop-shaped
Niche remains empty, and the cherished
Commission is revoked. Soon children dub
Antonio *El Borrachón* as he reels
About Bexar in the fumes of popskull
Caribbean rum. The padres bury him
In the earthen floor of the nave, just beyond
The sacristy's groined vault. Already
The groundwater is rising through porous stone.

II. Gone To Texas: Micajah Autry

Booking passage on the steamboat *Pacific*
One evening in early December 1835,
Micajah Autry scarcely envisions
His death before the blood-spackled façade
Of Antonio's deft conceiving, how he
And a beleaguered few would rally
In the shadow of that ruined proscenium
With no thought for the plaudits of the many,
The vast afflatus of the *Telegraph and*
Texas Register: "Spirits of the mighty,
Though fallen! Honors and rest are with ye."
Smoke batting its tall stacks, the stern-wheeler
Churns the Mississippi midchannel,
The moon shattered gypsum in its wake.

III. The 1836 Siege: Micajah Autry

Micajah owns a rich tenor voice, a sheaf
Of unpublished verse. He joins Crockett
On the long trek to Bexar, where the garrison
Scorns drill, holds formations in the cantina—
Almeron Dickinson, a blacksmith from Tennessee,
Forges horseshoes on a twin-pronged anvil.
Micajah savors the hammer's rhythmic pitch,
The prolonged hiss as incandescent iron
Cools out of its element to a new hardness:
Were ever words so malleable, so concise?
But winter settles in, cold and drizzling,
No time for poetry. At forty-two,
His thighbone grips his knee like fire tongs.
The weather eases up within a week.

Micajah shuns fandangos, and quarters
In the Alamo. Each night he guards
The horses cut out to graze on dry mesquite.
Three days before Santa Anna's arrival,
A ripple runs through the *caballada*,
The eyes of mustangs opalescent fire
Beneath the Comanche moon. Such portents
Go unheeded, till Bonham spurs in
From La Bahía, his Appaloosa
Blown and lathered, slick with yeasty silver.
Travis replies to the demand for surrender
With a cannon shot; the eighteen-pounder's
Bull-throated roar breaks and rolls like thunder—
Even at Washington-on-the-Brazos.

Politicians bickering in conclave
Pause to listen. But you knew, Micajah,
Didn't you, in the pith and marrow
Of your bones, that no relief column
Would move toward Bexar? On March first,
When thirty men slip the icy fetters
Of Cibolo Creek and follow the starlit
Acequia to the south gate, Travis
Slits an ox's throat to honor the town
Of Gonzales, searing the chine and joints
Over flame-gutted sticks of poplar.
That night, Micajah partakes of eternity
As he crouches in a weathered portico
On the plaza. Ramon Caro, official

Secretary to His Supreme Excellency,
Would later call the Alamo "a mere
Corral, and nothing more." In the predawn
Haze and powdersmoke of the final battle,
Micajah falls back on the chapel,
His shotgun charged with blue whistlers
That cut a young *soldado*'s plain coatee
To gaudy regimentals. The poet's breath
Catches in his beard, his right lung crumpled
By a musket ball: a bayonet gleans
The remnant, a twitch like phantom
Nerves in a severed limb. All afternoon
The Jimenez *cazadores* trundle
Cartloads of rebel corpses to pyres

Heaped on the Alameda. At last
The sun relents, melting down the brass
Shield insignia of bullrush-tufted shakos.
Parched and weary *soldados* loosen
And slough their glittering chin scales.
One by one, with a blazing pitch pine knot,
The bonfires are lit, the wind springs up…

Columns of smoke and heat-flaked bone stand in heaven.

Acknowledgments

The utter futility of attempting to acknowledge everyone involved in the making of this book appears more daunting each time I ponder the matter, but I must nevertheless endeavor to do so. First of all, I am indebted to Hope Maxwell-Snyder, whose Somondoco Press provides a splendid forum for all genres of the literary arts, from poetry, fiction, and drama, to personal memoir. May her vision and enterprise continue to thrive and prosper. Secondly, I wish to thank Brandon Cornwell; his skills as both compositor and designer seem more than commensurate to every task placed before him. I must also recognize those who endorsed the product of my labors while it still lay in manuscript, in particular Keith Alexander, William Chemerka, Andrew Ciotola, Scott Ely, Stephen Harrigan, Kevin and Mary Hendryx, William Page, Michael Waters, Nicholas Wellman, and Richard Wooten. Special thanks go out to Peter Stitt and George Core, who not only encouraged, but also nurtured this project along at every stage of development. To the librarians and staff of the D.R.T. Library, grateful acknowledgment is forthcoming for allowing me access to both their general holdings and special archives. Words cannot hope to convey my heartfelt gratitude to my wife Caroline for her loving and patient support in more things than this. And lastly, I thank my father, who took me by the hand to the Strand Theatre in Memphis one rainy Sunday night in early spring of 1961.